# A Calendar *of* I

*Thirty Contemporary Hymns*
*for Seasons of the Christian Year*

TIMOTHY DUDLEY-SMITH

music editor:
WILLIAM LLEWELLYN

music engraver:
ANDREW PARKER

# CANTERBURY
## PRESS

Norwich

# CONTENTS

Where, throughout the collection, suggested alternative tunes contain a
cross-reference, the letters *CP* signify *Common Praise,* SCM-Canterbury Press, 2000

# 1   Awake, as in the skies above

FRITH HILL   CM

George A. Robinson c. 1840–1909

Alternative tunes: ST MAGNUS (Clarke) *(CP 172)*, IRISH *(CP 608)*

AWAKE, as in the skies above
  the darkness yields to dawn;
so came God's gift of light and love,
  our Saviour Christ was born.

2   Awake and watch!  The hour draws on
   of his return to reign;
our night of sin and sorrow gone
   when Christ shall come again.

3   Awake from sleep, from time and place
   to God's eternal now,
when every eye shall see his face
   and every knee shall bow.

4   Behold the Sun of Righteousness
   whose glories blaze abroad,
till every tongue on earth confess
   that Jesus Christ is Lord!

# 2   The God of whom the prophets told

HERONGATE   LM

English traditional melody
*arranged* Ralph Vaughan Williams 1872–1958

Alternative tune: CHURCH TRIUMPHANT *(CP 349)*

THE God of whom the prophets told,
  when truth in signs and visions came,
we now in Christ by faith behold
  and hear his word and know his Name.

2 That Name the ransomed glorify,
  by God redeemed, a burning brand,
the apple of our Maker's eye,
  the jewels shining in his hand.

3 No longer shepherdless we roam,
  the flock for whom the Saviour died,
the Lord shall make with us his home
  and be our light at eventide.

4 His grace alone our confidence,
  his Spirit's power about our ways,
a wall of fire our sure defence,
  his covenant our song of praise.

5 Rejoice! for Christ shall come again,
  with peace and righteousness restored:
from sea to sea our King shall reign,
  and all be holy to the Lord.

*based on images from the book of Zechariah*

# 3   Light to the world, a child is born

DREAM ANGUS   8 8 10 9

Scottish traditional melody
*arranged* William Llewellyn *b.* 1925

LIGHT to the world, a child is born;
    dark is the night before the dawn:
day is upon us, darkness is dying,
with Mary's child in slumber lying.

    *Christ has come, our life to share;*
    *sorrows and sins and griefs to bear:*
    *see where above us the heavens are clear,*
    *the angels are singing for Christ is here!*

2    Light for a world gone far astray,
    dawn of the hope of God's new day;
    songs for our sighing, joy for our weeping,
    with Mary's child so softly sleeping.

    *Christ has come, our life to share;*
    *sorrows and sins and griefs to bear:*
    *see where above us the heavens are clear,*
    *the daylight is breaking for Christ is here!*

3    Light of the world, God's only Son!
    . now is the day of grace begun:
    love is among us, love beyond dreaming,
    with Mary's child for our redeeming.

    *Christ has come, our life to share;*
    *sorrows and sins and griefs to bear:*
    *see where above us the heavens are clear,*
    *the darkness is ended for Christ is here!*

# 4    Carols to Christ be sung

MOSCOW    664 6664           Melody by Felice de Giardini 1716–1796

CAROLS to Christ be sung,
joy be on every tongue,
   welcome his birth!
where in the starry sky
legions of angels cry
'Glory to God on high,
   peace upon earth'.

2   Shepherds behold the sight,
keeping their flocks by night,
   safe till the morn:
down through the dark they tread,
finding the cattle-shed,
where in a manger bed
   Jesus is born.

3   Kings from the East arise,
worshippers strange and wise,
   journeying far;
incense and gold they bring,
gifts for a God and King,
myrrh for his suffering,
   led by a star.

4   Though, like the star that shone,
shepherds and kings are gone
   long past recall,
he who by faith is known,
Saviour and Son alone,
reigns from his Father's throne,
   Christ over all!

# 5  'Glory to the God of heaven'

EVANGELISTS  887 D

Melody in J. B. König's *Harmonische Lieder,* 1738
Harmony from J. S. Bach 1685–1750
based on a chorale by Johann Löhner 1645–1705

'GLORY to the God of heaven,
  peace on earth to mortals given':
hear again the angel's voice!
Promised hope of every nation,
Christ has come for our salvation,
  let the waiting world rejoice!

2  Word of God beyond our telling,
Son of God with sinners dwelling,
  God appears in human frame:
flesh and blood their Maker borrows,
born to bear our griefs and sorrows,
  who as Love incarnate came.

3  Love enshrined in infant tender,
blazoned forth in heaven's splendour,
  King of love to earth come down:
God in Christ among us living,
tasting death for our forgiving,
  bowed beneath a thorny crown.

4  To this child of our salvation
join the songs of adoration,
  hear again the angels' cry!
Christ is risen, Christ ascended,
all our sins and sorrows ended:
  Glory be to God Most High!

5  Words: © Timothy Dudley-Smith in Europe (including UK and Ireland) and Africa, and in the rest of the world © 2006 by Hope Publishing Company.

# 6   The promised Light of all the earth

STRACATHRO   CM

from *Christian Vespers,* 1832
Charles Hutcheson 1792–1860

Alternative tunes: ST TIMOTHY *(CP 5)*, STOCKTON *(CP 533)*

THE promised Light of all the earth
    is sprung from David's line,
and in his long-awaited birth
    salvation's glories shine.

2    We share by faith the gift of grace
        to favoured Simeon given,
    who saw his Saviour's infant face
        and blessed the God of heaven.

3    We know, what he foresaw in part,
        the coming cross and grave,
    a sword to pierce through Mary's heart,
        a life laid down to save.

4    So we with Anna stand and bless
        and lift our hearts above,
    to tell in praise and thankfulness
        of God's redeeming love.

5    O Lord our God, we here present
        our sacrifice of praise,
    and offer up the life you lent,
        the service of our days.

6    Be ours the risen Christ to know
        who to his Temple came,
    that meeting him we live and grow
        and glory in his Name.

*based on Luke 2.22-38*

# 7  When John baptized by Jordan's river

RENDEZ À DIEU    98 98 D          Melody probably by Louis Bourgeois *c.*1510–1561
                                   as in *Genevan Psalter,* 1543

WHEN John baptized by Jordan's river
    in faith and hope the people came,
that John and Jordan might deliver
    their troubled souls from sin and shame.
They came to seek a new beginning,
    the human spirit's ageless quest,
repentance, and an end of sinning,
    renouncing every wrong confessed.

2   There as the Lord, baptized and praying,
        rose from the stream, the sinless one,
    a voice was heard from heaven saying,
        'This is my own beloved Son.'
    There as the Father's word was spoken,
        not in the power of wind and flame,
    but of his love and peace the token,
        seen as a dove, the Spirit came.

3   O Son of Man, our nature sharing,
        in whose obedience all are blest,
    Saviour, our sins and sorrows bearing,
        hear us and grant us this request:
    daily to grow, by grace defended,
        filled with the Spirit from above;
    in Christ baptized, beloved, befriended,
        children of God in peace and love.

# 8  Our Saviour Christ once knelt in prayer

ST MATTHIAS    88 88 88

William Henry Monk 1823–1889

Alternative tune: SURREY *(CP 412)*

OUR Saviour Christ once knelt in prayer
   with none but three disciples there,
upon a lonely mountain high
beneath a blue expanse of sky:
   below them, far as eye could see,
   the little hills of Galilee.

2   There as he prays a radiance bright
transfigures all his form to light;
his robe in dazzling splendour shows
a purer white than sunlit snows,
   while on his countenance divine
   transcendent glories burn and shine.

3   So for a moment stands revealed
what human form and flesh concealed;
while Moses and Elijah share
in earth and heaven mingled there,
   with him whom prophecy foresaw,
   the true fulfiller of the law.

4   The shadowed summit, wrapped in cloud,
sounds to a voice that echoes loud:
'This is my true beloved Son,
listen to him, my chosen one.'
   The glory fades. With all its pains
   the road to Calvary remains.

5   Give to us, Lord, the eyes to see
as saw those first disciples three:
a teacher true, a friend indeed,
the risen Saviour sinners need,
   the Son whose praise eternal rings,
   the Lord of lords and King of kings!

*based on Mark 9.2-10*

# 9 Christ our Redeemer knew temptation's hour

FORECOURT   10 10 10 10

William Llewellyn b. 1925

1 Christ our Re-deem-er knew temp-ta-tion's hour____ in de-sert pla-ces, si-lent and a-part; and three times o-ver met the temp-ter's power with

God's word\_ writ - ten, hid - den in his heart.

Alternative tune: ELLERS *(14)*

CHRIST our Redeemer knew temptation's hour
    in desert places, silent and apart;
and three times over met the tempter's power
    with God's word written, hidden in his heart.

2    He makes not bread what God has made a stone,
    he at whose bidding water turns to wine:
we are not meant to live by bread alone
    but as God speaks the word of life divine.

3    He will not ask the fickle crowd's acclaim,
    nor flaunt the Sonship which is his by right,
nor seem distrustful of the Father's Name
    who bids us walk by faith and not by sight.

4    He seeks no kingdom but by cross and grave,
    for love of sinners spurning Satan's throne:
his triumph seen in those he died to save
    who, to his glory, worship God alone.

# 10  O Christ, who faced in deserts bare

BARTON SPRINGS    88 88 88

Peter Cutts *b.* 1937

1 O Christ, who faced in des-erts bare the fier-cest test temp-ta-tion brings, to win for us a pas-ture fair and wa-ter from e-ter-nal springs: now, lest our feet be led a-stray, Good

Shep‑herd, walk with us_____ to‑day.

Alternative tune: VATER UNSER *(CP 452)*, COLCHESTER (Wesley) *(CP 117)*

O CHRIST, who faced in deserts bare
  the fiercest test temptation brings,
to win for us a pasture fair
    and water from eternal springs:
      now, lest our feet be led astray,
      Good Shepherd, walk with us today.

2   We know the voice that calls our name,
      the patient, low, insistent word;
    a voice, for evermore the same,
      that James and John and Peter heard:
        to follow where their steps have gone,
        Good Shepherd, lead your people on.

3   For all your scattered flock we pray,
      whose eyes the Lamb of God behold;
    come as their true and living Way
      to other sheep of every fold:
        from powers of sin and death and grave,
        Good Shepherd, stoop to seek and save.

4   Good Shepherd of the life laid down,
      Great Shepherd of the ransom paid,
    that life, and glory, and a crown,
      be ours, in righteousness arrayed:
        our ways direct, our wants provide,
        Good Shepherd, still be guard and guide.

5   Teach us to journey here below
      as those who seek their rest above,
    and daily by your grace to grow
      in truth and holiness and love:
        and when our pilgrim days are past,
        Good Shepherd, bring us home at last.

# 11 No tramp of soldiers' marching feet

O.B.S.   DCM

Peter Crook b. 1954

1 No tramp of sol – diers' march – ing feet with ban – ners and with drums, no sound of mu – sic's mar – tial beat: 'The King of glo – ry comes!' To greet what pomp of king – ly pride no bells in tri – umph ring, no ci – ty

1  NO tramp of soldiers' marching feet
      with banners and with drums,
   no sound of music's martial beat:
      'The King of glory comes!'
   To greet what pomp of kingly pride
   no bells in triumph ring,
   no city gates swing open wide:
      'Behold, behold your King!'

2  And yet he comes. The children cheer;
   with palms his path is strown.
   With every step the cross draws near:
      the King of glory's throne.
   Astride a colt he passes by
   as loud hosannas ring,
   or else the very stones would cry
      'Behold, behold your King!'

3  What fading flowers his road adorn;
   the palms, how soon laid down!
   No bloom or leaf but only thorn
      the King of glory's crown.
   The soldiers mock, the rabble cries,
   the streets with tumult ring,
   as Pilate to the mob replies,
      'Behold, behold your King!'

4  Now he who bore for mortals' sake
   the cross and all its pains
   and chose a servant's form to take,
      the King of glory reigns.
   Hosanna to the Saviour's Name
   till heaven's rafters ring,
   and all the ransomed host proclaim
      'Behold, behold your King!'

# 12 In the same night in which he was betrayed

TRAITOR'S KISS  10 10 10 10 10 10

Martin Setchell *b.* 1949

Alternative tunes: SONG 1 *(CP 181i)*, UNDE ET MEMORES *(CP 559)*

**12**  Music: © Kevin Mayhew Ltd, Buxhall, Stowmarket, Suffolk. IP14 3BW. Used by permission

IN the same night in which he was betrayed,
 the supper ended, and the dark come down,
there in that lonely garden Jesus prayed,
  beyond the lamplight of the sleeping town:
   above the trees the Paschal moon is high,
   the olive branches black against the sky.

2 What agony of spirit bowed his head
  lies far beyond our human heart to frame;
yet 'Not my will but yours' at last he said,
  as lights and torches through the garden came:
   so Judas ends what love of self began,
   and with a kiss betrays the Son of Man.

3 The hour is come: the power of darkness reigns.
  See, like a lamb, the Lord is led away.
Of twelve disciples only one remains
  to wait the dawning of the final day:
   alone before his captors Jesus stands,
   while in the courtyard Peter warms his hands.

*  *  *

4 Turn, Lord, and look: for many a cock has crowed;
  we too betray, forsake you, or deny.
For us, like Peter, bitter tears have flowed,
  lost in the dark, no language but a cry;
   a cry of weakness, failure and despair:
   Lord, in your mercy, stoop to hear our prayer.

# 13   An upper room with evening lamps ashine

SURSUM CORDA   10 10 10 10          Alfred Morton Smith 1879–1971

Alternative tune: ELLERS *(14)*

AN upper room with evening lamps ashine,
   the twelve disciples, and the table spread;
now in our turn Christ bids us pour the wine,
   and in remembrance bless and break the bread.

2    We see by faith upon the cross displayed
      his body broken and his blood outpoured;
in that dread robe of majesty arrayed
      we gaze in worship on the dying Lord.

3    Dead for our sins, yet reigning now above,
      still to our hearts we find his presence given;
take for ourselves the pledges of his love,
      foretaste and token of that feast in heaven.

4    So send us out to love and serve and praise,
      filled with his Spirit, as the Master said:
love, joy and peace the wine of all our days,
      Christ and his life our true and living bread.

# 14 As in that upper room you left your seat

ELLERS  10 10 10 10

Edward John Hopkins 1818–1901
*harmonised* Arthur Seymour Sullivan 1842–1900

Alternative tune: SURSUM CORDA *(13)*

AS in that upper room you left your seat
    and took a towel and chose a servant's part,
so for today, Lord, wash again my feet,
    who in your mercy died to cleanse my heart.

2  I bow before you, all my sin confessed,
        to hear again the words of love you said;
    and at your table, as your honoured guest,
        I take and eat the true and living bread.

3  So in remembrance of your life laid down
        I come to praise you for your grace divine;
    saved by your cross, and subject to your crown,
        strengthened for service by this bread and wine.

# 15   A purple robe, a crown of thorn

A PURPLE ROBE   86 86 Triple

David Wilson *b.* 1940
*arranged* Noël Tredinnick *b.* 1949

1 A pur-ple robe, a crown of thorn, a reed in his___ right
4 He hangs, by whom the world was made, be-neath the dark-ened

hand;_____ be-fore the sol-diers' spite and scorn I
sky;_____ the ev-er-last-ing ran-som paid, I

see my Sa-viour stand._____ 2 He bears be-tween_ the
see my Sa-viour die._____ 5 He shares on high_ his

Ro-man guard the weight of all___ our woe;_____ a
Fa-ther's throne, who once in mer-cy came;_____ for

stum - bling fi - gure bowed and scarred I see my Sa - viour
all his love to sin - ners shown I sing my Sa - viour's

*Fine*

go. 3 Fast to the cross - 's spread - ing span,
Name.

high in the sun - lit air, all the un - num - bered

*D.C. al Fine*

sins of man I see my Sa - viour bear.

# 16  Approach with awe this holiest place

PALMYRA   86 86 88                                      Joseph Summers 1843–1916

Alternative tune: AUCH JETZT MACHT GOTT

APPROACH with awe this holiest place,
the last of death's domain;
the shuttered heavens hide their face,
the powers of darkness reign;
for there beneath those sombre skies
the Prince of life, forsaken, dies.

2 The Prince of life! For us he came
from that high throne above,
his cross the measure of our shame,
his death the price of love;
and at his cross, my soul, begin
to feel the weight of love and sin.

3 Can this poor broken form be he
who taught the words of truth,
who strode the hills of Galilee
in all the flower of youth?
Can this be he, this lifeless head,
with grace and strength and beauty fled?

4 By wood and nails the work is done
that answers all our need,
the prize of full salvation won,
the ransomed sinner freed.
Draw near with faith, my soul, and see
the Prince of life who died for me.

5 The Prince of life! While time shall last
his cross and grave remain
sure signs of sin and sorrow past,
bright morning come again:
an empty cross, an empty grave,
a risen Christ to seek and save!

# 17  Behold, as love made manifest

BELMONT  CM

Melody by William Gardiner 1770–1853
*harmonised* Compilers of *Revised Church Hymnary*, 1927

Alternative tune: BALLERMA *(CP 221ii)*

BEHOLD, as love made manifest,
   the Lamb of God divine:
redeeming love perceived, possessed,
   in sacrifice and sign;

2    A sign of saving grace displayed,
      a sign of sinners' worth;
    by wood and nails a ransom paid
      for all the sins of earth.

3    A sign of love beyond belief,
      where every failing breath
    affirms through agony and grief
      a love that conquers death;

4    A sign of mercy's wide extent
      and universal sway;
    the evil powers of darkness spent
      for Christ has won the day.

5    A sign of triumph over sin
      and dread devouring grave,
    a sign of all he died to win
      for all he longs to save;

6    Herein is love beyond all price,
      the Lamb of God divine:
    his all-sufficient sacrifice,
      his all-prevailing sign.

17  Words: © Timothy Dudley-Smith in Europe (including UK and Ireland) and Africa, and in the rest of the world © 1984 by Hope Publishing Company.

# 18    Christ is the shining sun of all our days

HIGHLAND CATHEDRAL    10 10 10 10        Uli Roever and Michael Korb
*arranged* Compilers of *Church Hymnary, 4th edition* 2005

CHRIST is the shining sun of all our days,
    his is the touch that sets the stars ablaze;
sight to the eyes that but for him were blind,
Christ is the Light of every Christian mind.

2    Christ is the Love of God to mortals shown,
Saviour and Shepherd come to claim his own;
Christ our Redeemer, at whose feet we fall;
Love of the Father at the heart of all.

3    Christ is the Life who gave himself to save;
lifeless he lay within the silent grave.
See!  as the Easter dawn dispels the gloom,
Jesus is risen!  he has burst the tomb!

4    Christ is the victor over death's domains;
Christ is the King who now in glory reigns.
Jesus is Lord!  and to his Name be praise:
he is the shining sun of all our days.

# 19 All shall be well

SONG 46   10 10

Melody and bass by Orlando Gibbons 1583–1625

ALL shall be well!
 for on our Easter skies
see Christ the Sun
 of Righteousness arise.

2 All shall be well!
the sacrifice is made;
the sinner freed,
 the price of pardon paid.

3 All shall be well!
the cross and passion past;
dark night is done,
 bright morning come at last.

4 All shall be well!
within our Father's plan
death has no more
 dominion over man.

5 Jesus alive!
Rejoice and sing again,
'All shall be well
 for evermore, Amen!'

# 20i Christ is risen as he said

CHRIST IS RISEN AS HE SAID   77 77

John Carter *b.*1930

1 Christ is ris - en as he said,
Christ the first born from the dead: 2 See, the stone is
rolled a - way, see the place where Je - sus lay.

glo - ri - fied. risen, a - scend - ed, glo - ri - fied.

CHRIST is risen as he said,
    Christ the firstborn from the dead:

2    See, the stone is rolled away,
      see the place where Jesus lay.

3    Lord of life, he lives again;
      Lord of lords, to rule and reign:

4    Every tongue confess him now,
      every knee before him bow.

5    Christ who died our life to win,
      Christ has conquered death and sin:

6    Now is all his warfare done,
      now is every triumph won.

7    Son of God, his life he gave,
      Son of Man, to seek and save:

8    Risen now, the Son who died,
      risen, ascended, glorified.

# 20 ii  Christ is risen as he said

LAUDS   77 77

John Wilson 1905–1992

Flowing easily

(vv. 1, 3, 5, 7)

(vv. 2, 4, 6, 8)

(small notes Organ only)

CHRIST is risen as he said,
  Christ the firstborn from the dead:

2  See, the stone is rolled away,
    see the place where Jesus lay.

3  Lord of life, he lives again;
    Lord of lords, to rule and reign:

4  Every tongue confess him now,
    every knee before him bow.

5  Christ who died our life to win,
    Christ has conquered death and sin:

6  Now is all his warfare done,
    now is every triumph won.

7  Son of God, his life he gave,
    Son of Man, to seek and save:

8  Risen now, the Son who died,
    risen, ascended, glorified.

# 21  Jesus, Prince and Saviour

ST GERTRUDE   65 65 D and refrain                    Arthur Seymour Sullivan 1842–1900

JESUS, Prince and Saviour,
  Lord of life who died,
  Christ, the friend of sinners,
mocked and crucified;
for a world's salvation
he his body gave,
lay at last death's victim
lifeless in the grave.
  *Lord of life triumphant,*
  *risen now to reign!*
  *King of endless ages,*
  *Jesus lives again!*

2    In his power and Godhead
every victory won,
pain and passion ended,
all his purpose done:
Christ the Lord is risen!
sighs and sorrows past,
death's dark night is over,
morning comes at last!

3    Resurrection morning,
sinners' bondage freed!
Christ the Lord is risen,
he is risen indeed!
Jesus, Prince and Saviour,
Lord of life who died,
Christ the King of glory
now is glorified!

# 22 The final triumph won

MILLENNIUM    66 66 88

Twelve Psalm and Hymn Tunes, c. 1814
Joseph Major *fl.* 1814

THE final triumph won,
  the full atonement made,
salvation's work is done,
  redemption's price is paid:
    the morning breaks, the dark is fled,
    for Christ is risen from the dead!

2  The tomb in which he lay
     lies empty now and bare;
   the stone is rolled away,
     no lifeless form is there:
       the sting is drawn from death and grave,
       for Christ is risen, strong to save!

3  For us the Saviour died,
     with us he lives again,
   to God the Father's side
     exalted now to reign:
       to throne and crown by right restored,
       for Christ is risen, Christ is Lord!

4  As one with him we rise
     to seek the things above,
   in life that never dies,
     in righteousness and love:
       let praise unite our ransomed powers,
       for Christ is risen, Christ is ours!

# 23   Christ high-ascended, now in glory seated

CHRISTE SANCTORUM   11 11 11 6

Melody from *Paris Antiphoner*, 1681
*arranged* John Wilson 1905–1992

*Unison* or *Harmony*

CHRIST high-ascended, now in glory seated,
throned and exalted, victory completed,
death's dread dominion finally defeated,
  we are his witnesses.

2 Christ from the Father every power possessing,
who on his chosen lifted hands in blessing,
sends forth his servants, still in faith confessing,
  we are his witnesses.

3 Christ, who in dying won for us salvation,
lives now the first-born of the new creation;
to win disciples out of every nation,
  we are his witnesses.

4 Christ in his splendour, all dominion gaining,
Christ with his people evermore remaining,
Christ to all ages gloriously reigning,
  we are his witnesses.

5 As at his parting, joy shall banish grieving,
faith in his presence strengthen our believing;
filled with his Spirit, love and power receiving,
  we are his witnesses.

# 24  Risen Lord in splendour seated

REGENT SQUARE    87 87 87

Henry Thomas Smart 1813–1879

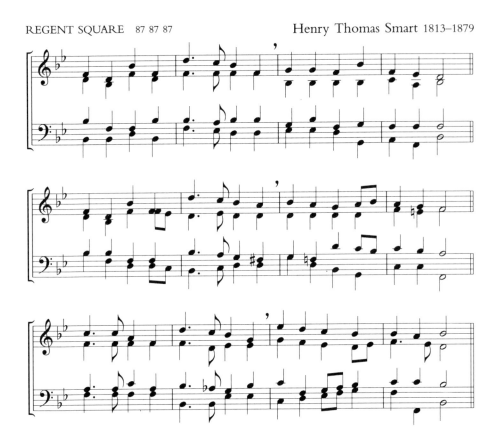

Alternative tune: RHUDDLAN *(CP 356)*

RISEN Lord in splendour seated,
  throned at God the Father's side,
Prince of life who death defeated,
Lamb who once for sinners died,
  Christ for ever Son and Saviour
reigns in triumph glorified.

2  He who came our nature bearing,
child of earth from heaven's throne,
human trials and troubles sharing,
God himself in flesh made known,
  Christ for ever with his people
sends his Spirit on his own.

3  Love of God, unwearied, reaching
furthest bounds of time and space,
still by foolishness of preaching
holding forth the word of grace,
  Christ for ever interceding
builds his church in every place.

4  Earth awaits her new creation
when from sin and death restored,
in the strength of full salvation
Christ is honoured and adored,
  Christ for ever high ascended,
sovereign, universal Lord!

# 25  Spirit of God within me

WILLOW RIVER   76 86 86 86

Michael Joncas *b.* 1951

1 Spi - rit of God with - in __ me, pos - sess my hu - man frame; _____ fan the dull em - bers of my heart, stir up the liv - ing __ flame. _____ Strive till that im - age A - dam lost, new mint - - ed and re - stored, in shin - ing splen - dour bright-ly bears the like-ness of the Lord.

SPIRIT of God within me,
  possess my human frame;
fan the dull embers of my heart,
  stir up the living flame.
Strive till that image Adam lost,
  new minted and restored,
in shining splendour brightly bears
  the likeness of the Lord.

2   Spirit of truth within me,
    possess my thought and mind;
lighten anew the inward eye
   by Satan rendered blind;
shine on the words that wisdom speaks
   and grant me power to see
the truth made known to all in Christ,
   and in that truth be free.

3   Spirit of love within me,
    possess my hands and heart;
break through the bonds of self-concern
   that seeks to stand apart:
grant me the love that suffers long,
   that hopes, believes and bears,
the love fulfilled in sacrifice,
   that cares as Jesus cares.

4   Spirit of life within me,
    possess this life of mine;
come as the wind of heaven's breath,
   come as the fire divine!
Spirit of Christ, the living Lord,
   reign in this house of clay,
till from its dust with Christ I rise
   to everlasting day.

Alternative tune: ALFORD (adapted) *(CP 196)*

# 26 When God the Spirit came

VINEYARD HAVEN    66 86 66

Richard Wayne Dirksen 1921–2003

WHEN God the Spirit came
 upon his church outpoured
in sound of wind and sign of flame
they spread his truth abroad,
 and filled with the Spirit
proclaimed that Christ is Lord.

2 What courage, power and grace
that youthful church displayed!
to those of every tribe and race
they witnessed unafraid,
 and filled with the Spirit
they broke their bread and prayed.

3 They saw God's word prevail,
his kingdom still increase,
no part of all his purpose fail,
no promised blessing cease,
 and filled with the Spirit
knew love and joy and peace.

4 Their theme was Christ alone,
the Lord who lived and died,
who rose to his eternal throne
at God the Father's side;
 and filled with the Spirit
the church was multiplied.

5 So to this present hour
our task is still the same,
in pentecostal love and power
his gospel to proclaim,
 and filled with the Spirit,
rejoice in Jesus' Name.

# 27　Be present, Spirit of the Lord

NEWCASTLE (Morley)　86 88 6

Henry L. Morley *b.c.* 1835
from *The London Tune Book,* 1875

Alternative tune: REPTON *(CP 411)*

BE present, Spirit of the Lord,
  let sounds of earth be dumb;
the Father's love be shed abroad,
the dew of blessing on us poured:
  O silent Spirit, come!

2  In power unseen upon us rest,
    your gracious gifts impart:
  a mind renewed, a spirit blessed,
  a life where Christ is manifest,
    an understanding heart.

3  Love's sovereign work of grace fulfil,
    our souls to Christ incline,
  intent to do the Father's will
  and stand by faith before him still
    in righteousness divine.

4  O Spirit come, and with us stay;
    make every heart your home.
  So work in us that we who pray
  may walk with Christ in wisdom's way:
    O Holy Spirit, come!

# 28  Affirm anew the threefold Name

ELLACOMBE  DCM

German melody, 18th century
as adapted in Mainz *Gesangbuch*, 1833
*harmonised* St Gallen *Gesangbuch*, 1863

Alternative tune: TYROL *(CP 200)*

AFFIRM anew the threefold Name
  of Father, Spirit, Son,
our God whose saving acts proclaim
  a world's salvation won.
In him alone we live and move
  and breath and being find,
the wayward children of his love
  who cares for humankind.

2  Declare in all the earth his grace,
    to every heart his call,
the living Lord of time and place
    whose love embraces all.
So shall his endless praise be sung,
    his teaching truly heard,
and every culture, every tongue,
    receive his timeless word.

3  Confirm our faith in this our day
    amid earth's shifting sand,
with Christ as Life and Truth and Way,
    a Rock on which to stand;
the one eternal Son and Lord
    by God the Father given,
the true and life-imparting Word,
    the Way that leads to heaven.

4  Renew once more the ancient fire,
    let love our hearts inflame;
renew, restore, unite, inspire
    the church that bears your Name;
one Name exalted over all,
    one Father, Spirit, Son,
O grant us grace to heed your call
    and in that Name be one.

# 29  Here within this house of prayer

DIX   77 77 77

from a chorale by
Conrad Kocher 1786–1872
*arranged* William Henry Monk 1823–1889

HERE within this house of prayer
all our Father's love declare;
love that gave us birth, and planned
days and years beneath his hand:
　　praise to God whose love and power
　　bring us to this present hour!

2　Here, till earthly praises end,
tell of Christ the sinner's friend;
Christ whose blood for us was shed,
Lamb of God and living bread,
　　life divine and truth and way,
　　light of everlasting day.

3　Here may all our faint desire
feel the Spirit's wind and fire,
souls that sleep the sleep of death
stir to life beneath his breath:
　　may his power upon us poured
　　send us out to serve the Lord!

4　Here may faith and love increase,
flowing forth in joy and peace
from the Father, Spirit, Son,
undivided, Three-in-One:
　　his the glory all our days
　　in this house of prayer and praise!

# 30 Give thanks to God, and honour those

ST MATTHEW DCM

*A Supplement to the New Version,* 1708
probably by William Croft 1678–1727

GIVE thanks to God, and honour those
    whose fame was spread abroad,
whose well-remembered lives disclose
    the glories of their Lord;
who held their just and gentle sway
    in trust beneath his hand,
and humbly sought to serve their day
    and work what God had planned.

2    His Name they lived to glorify
      who gives the poet's word,
the painter's all-discerning eye,
    the soul by music stirred;
and high among the human skills
    of wisdom, science, art,
a virtue grace alone instils,
    the pastor's patient heart.

3    For teacher's gift, for prophet's fire,
      for preachers of the word,
for all who still our souls inspire
    we praise your Name, O Lord;
we seek to follow where they trod,
    to reap what they have sown,
who spent themselves for love of God
    and sought his praise alone.

4    And some there be who take their rest
      in unremembered graves,
whose names are numbered with the blest
    whom Jesus loves and saves;
who kept the faith, who ran the race,
    whose work on earth is done:
may we, their children, know your grace
    until the crown is won.

*based on Ecclesiasticus 44.1-15*

30   Words: © Timothy Dudley-Smith in Europe (including UK and Ireland) and Africa, and in the rest of the world © 1999 by Hope Publishing Company.

# Index of Tunes